My Africa

Copyright
2023
Noah Ras

To my Parents

My Africa

The River of Life

It was the best times of my life, and it was the worst times. Father said, justice is in the afterlife, in this life, there is none. My name is Joseph. In my family there were seven children, four boys and three girls. I am the second born and the second son. I was fond of my brothers and sisters, and they were fond of me.

My younger brother and sister that came after me died at a very young age when I was still a young boy. I am not sure how they died. Things like that were not uncommon in the very difficult life in our village. The village was plagued with enormous malaria carrying insects, born in its rivers and water-ways, and beasts that rip children from their beds and steal them away into the night.

Many different kinds of creatures used to alight on the window-sill and on the trees above that surrounded our house: large, small, dark, green, and yellow-red ones. Once in a while a fly would land on my nose, I would not try catch it, but I held my breath and stared at it in wonder. The little creature was for me a greeting from the land of fun and play.

Mother Nature did her work very well, even in my small village. In the spring the rains fell, and the crops grew, and in the summer the wind and sand blinded and covered us well. High over the village the clouds passed - dark ones, light ones, some like popcorn, some in the shapes of rabbits, snakes, sheep, fish, and even whales. At times, hail as large as an egg fell from the sky high above, and often, after the rain fell, a colorful rainbow stretched above our heads.

Mother said to thank God Almighty for taking the time to color the sky so well for us. At night the moon shone and the stars appeared. My father would say that every star is much larger than our Earth, but as light as Cotton Candy. That is why it is able to float in the heavens, and does not fall on our heads. But how could a star be larger than our Earth but has the lightness of Cotton Candy? It was all a great mystery to me. Truly there are in life some wondrous things, most especially in Africa.

I was born on the western plains of Africa. My birthplace was a large, dry, seemingly endless stretch of land where muscles of dark-skinned men labored together and worked overtime to face the challenges of a tough and harsh climate and often cut-throat political movements.

It was there on the 1st of May that my beautiful mother gave birth to me, not in a pasture of wildflowers and green-leafed trees, but instead in a small village of sculptured huts made from locally found materials.

During the dry season, my homeland was hotter than a dragon's breath. The land would have cracks in it like the back of my grandfather's hands, like a spider's web. But when the rains were plentiful, the landscape was covered with so much greens, and wildflowers and lush tree leaves thick as my beautiful mother's hair. In her arms I was protected, within a dwelling that was neatly laid out, along with many others in the village of Rindiao. There we were safe from harm by man or beast alike.

My people lived in houses made of mud; malleable clay that came up out of the ground and was formed by the hands of the men into a place of shelter and life-long memories.

Those who were rich, had far better homes, but the warmth inside my house is what made it special to me. My house had big rocks placed in a circle out in the yard. It was where the children would gather to listen to my uncle who would enthrall us with stories about God and His book. My house had only one tree out in the back yard. The shape of that tree is etched into my memory, as is the silhouette of my uncle surrounded by children sitting in the yard.

The best time of my life was when I was a child living in Rindiao with my family.

Looking back on my life now, I can see that all of my prayers were heard and answered, maybe not in the way that I wanted them to be, but God Almighty did answer.

There was safety and freedom for us to explore our homeland and her friendly people. We were carefree back then. As children, we spent many hours away from home each day. After we had finished helping our parents clean the house, we were free to play, run around exploring the surroundings, and experiencing the beauty of nature as only a boy or a child can appreciate.

My brothers, friends, and I fished in the rivers and played in the water channels which irrigated the many rice farms and fruit-bearing trees of mangos, bananas, guavas, lemons, and oranges.

There we had such liberty to feel the earth beneath our feet and to connect with nature. Shoes were a luxury that we just could not afford. I wore shorts and a shirt as I ran through the tough and rugged lands and its rivers. If I was lucky that day at the river, I would catch a fish to take home for my family. My mother would cook it for us and make me feel proud as she served it to all of us. I loved my family and was so happy I was able to help my father who worked so hard to provide all that he could for us.

We ate two meals a day. They were simple meals created out of what the surrounding earth offered to us. In the mornings for breakfast, we ate bread and something like coffee to dip it in. Our dinner was eaten out of a bowl filled with rice. And when possible we ate some fish stew.

In most villages like ours, catching a fish means surviving. This was certainly the case for my family. I learned early on that catching a fish was not always easy, but it was certainly a fun thing to do to pass the time as a young boy.

One morning after I had helped my mom clean the house, I went looking for my friends Traore and Lemine. I joined them on the banks of the river, and we decided the day was perfect for going fishing. Traore and Lemine had already made a fishing pole from some sticks, some strong thread, and an old hook. Although I was without any means to catch a fish, I decided to join them anyway. I thought to myself that when they took a rest, I would borrow one of their fishing poles and have a try at my luck casting into the river for a fish.

My plan did not materialize that day because they sat there all day and did not catch a single fish. However, things often happen in this life so fantastic that no imagination could have invented them.

I just was about to leave because I became bored waiting for a try at using one of their fishing poles, and it truly was such a beautiful, sunny day, so I ventured away for a walk on my own. My solo journey began by walking down the river and throwing some rocks into the surface that reflected a perfect sky. Above me the blue color and sun were flawless, not a single cloud in sight. An artist could not imagine having a better subject to use for a painting. I began a personal prayer and thanked God for being alive to enjoy such a great day.

My words of thanks had no more left my lips, when suddenly something very remarkable happened. An eagle dropped his catch, a large striped bass, on my head and then it fell to the ground. My natural instincts kicked in, and without thought, I jumped on it. It was a slippery thing, and it felt as though many minutes had passed as we were engaged in the battle of a lifetime; the poor fish was so desperate wanting to return to the water, and I was desperate for the opportunity to bring life-giving food back to my family.

Traore and Lemine heard the battle and commotion up on the river; they saw the struggle I was undergoing and came running to help. But fate was on my side and declared me victorious by the time my friends had arrived.

I had conquered this battle alone, and so I had this treasure to bring to my family. It was during her struggle for her last breath that my eldest brother Joshua had just come to the river. My brother did not like to see any creature suffering. He told me to release the fish back into the water, but it was already too late. Tears filled my eyes and slid down my face. I apologized to that brave fish and to my brother. I explained to the fish that her sacrifice would banish the gnawing hunger pains that come too often into our village and into our own home. I started to pray for the fish's soul. "Well, you have had your life. You have served your time in this world very well. You are no longer confined to this river; hungry, afraid, and sick, but now with God Himself. Who knows why you had to be a fish? But you were lucky for man is the worst sinner of all creatures."

With a grasp like a steel vice, I held the prize pressed into my chest, as I ran all the way back home to bring the divine gift to my mother.

My mother's face radiated with pride, joy and sincere thankfulness that the family would eat and that I was responsible for that gift. Quickly she began to work her magic to cook our meal. That night when my father, mother, brothers and sisters ate well, I was happy because when God offered me that gift, I was there to receive it. I offered another prayer of thanks that I was alive on such a beautiful day. On the weekends in the summertime, I often woke very early, so early that the sky was still glowing from the sunrise. To my father I made some pretext or other, put a few pieces of dry bread in my pockets to eat, and went off to meet Traore and Lemine to play or fish.

However, there were days when my brothers, friends and I would sit for hours on end on the riverbank trying to catch a single fish, but we never got one bite. If we were so lucky, we had a fishing pole ready to go. If not, we would fashion a rudimentary spear out of wood or slender branches and stand in the shallows of the river trying to spear a fish as it swam past us.

We would often splash about falling over, laughing at each other and sometimes catching a fish or two. They were slippery and, more often than not, they seemed to get away from us fast. Still we were able to contribute some fish to our families on some occasions, and everyone was always very grateful.

Feeding my parents and siblings was not the only reward that was gained from a day's fishing. Most often, fishing happens to take place amidst beautiful scenery. The willows around the river banks provided shade for all of us on those lazy days. Here, the bird life was also abundant with many different species that called these tall trees their home.

We would return home when the sun was setting slowly and peacefully on the horizon, turning the river glorious shades of blues, greens, and golds. These were truly special days for a young boy. One day my father gave me a fishing pole. To this day, I still remember how I happy I felt. I was so overjoyed that I went running to visit my friends to share my good fortune with them. We ran to the riverbank with our container filled with promises of another day of success. It seemed like we three stood at the edge of the river for the entire day, another beautiful day of clear skies and promise within our young lives, but no fish were hungry that day. That amazing sunny day seemed no different than other days, it was hot, and so all the fish lay quiet below the surface not to be enticed by our offerings of food to them.

As I looked into the sky another prayer slipped from my lips; and I thanked God for that amazing day. All of a sudden I realized that I was in the middle of the river! Something had pulled me quickly down and despite trying with all of my might, I could not pull my head out of the water. My grasp on the fishing pole was like a death-grip: I was not going to lose my fishing rod to this unseen creature trying to tear it away from me. My friends raced to help me, and managed to pull me out of the water while my hands still tightly gripped the fishing rod. I had no idea what was on the end of that fishing hook. I continued to fight for my fishing rod. My friends watched me struggle for many minutes with the pole, letting a little of the line out at a time and then reeling it back in, over and over again till the beast tired of our game. At last I reeled him in.

I saw something most extraordinary. It was truly an enormous fish, maybe as old as my grandfather. I would swear honestly, that the fish was as big as I was tall, but it was powerful with muscles like steel springs very tightly wound and bound, ready to leap out at any second. Once we were a little calmer, we began the difficult task of getting the huge fish home to my mother. At that moment, I heard my father calling my name. We tried to carry the fish, but it was too heavy for us. So I was empty-handed as I presented myself to my dad. My father's instructions were to bring medicine to my uncle who was very ill. "No fish?" father asked, "Well, maybe next time." I smiled and said, "Father, please go to edge of the river and see my surprise."

My dad began to walk towards the river; I thought that his strength was enough to carry home the fish to my mother, so I started off towards my uncle's house.

There are a few people in this world who are simply born good. Such was my uncle. In life there always lived a few men in every generation whom, Satan, could not corrupt or tempt to sin. My uncle was such a man. He had strong faith. No one could even distract him while he was reading or studying God's Book. He studied constantly. Summers and winters alike, he rose before sunrise and began to memorize and read. He was the greatest scholar in the whole village. At ten he had memorized God's Book in its entirety. By twelve, he had preached so many sermons, quoting from so many prophets that even the oldest among the scholars were pleased. You could hardly ask him a question that he could not answer.

The moment he entered his house, he ran straight to his books and began to leaf through them, sucking into his lungs so much ancient old dust. His lungs were swelling up and making it hard for the air to get through. He was ten years older than my father but fifteen years younger than his father. He and his father had grown old together, and the symptoms of old age were more apparent in my uncle than his own father; He lost most of his hair in his teens, and became stooped at very young age. He was thin, weak and tired most of the time. He loved mathematics, and was so passionate about religion, and soccer too.

His first wife, Sara, he fell in love with her at first sight. A year after her death, he was married again, and two years later, a third time. My grandmother loved him the most. Whenever my uncle became ill, my grandmother paced through his room for hours, praying in a sobbing chant. My uncle was loved by almost everyone. He had no enemies, and had good insight into practical things. Rachel, his third wife, and his final true love, was his best friend. Rachel was also married once or twice before. She was a simple, kind, and beautiful woman. She treated him with great respect. Although I was very young, I could see that he loved her a lot. Had it not been for Rachel, my uncle would have truly starved. He was too proud to ask for help, so she helped in whatever way possible. On Mondays, Rachel hired herself to a wealthy Berber family to wash their laundry, and on winter days went off to the woods to collect pecans off the ground, and to gather mushrooms, and berries too, as well as twigs, and pinecones for the stove. Rachel was also a great tailor.

When I returned from my uncle's house, my mother had prepared a wonderful meal. My mother was an excellent cook. Her face was glowing that day. My father hugged me and said: "Your fish was so big my son that I battled to bring it home to your mother." I was so pleased to know that I was able to bring home such a big prize to give to my family. We ate so well for the next few days, and because we were so blessed, my father invited our friends to share in our good fortune. We sat around the fire outside our home every night and listened to stories about the old days. For a very long time, each day I would go to the river, hoping to catch another big fish, but it was never as simple as that day to catch even a small fish.

When times were good at our house, I would get a penny or two from my father or mother. For me this penny, or Ouguya coin piece, represented all worldly pleasures. Near our house was Omar Sarra's bread and sweetshop, where one could buy candy squares (Guemou), cookies, and all sorts of sweets. An Ouguya was not nearly so large a coin as father and mother made it out to be. There were times when I was forced to trade a fish for a Guemou. One morning, I told my mother that I was going fishing. My mother smiled at me with wise assurance and told me it was a hot day and I might not catch a thing. I smiled back respectfully, and with boyish charm, and the confidence of someone who had already received a message directly from God Almighty, I said, "Today I will catch something big," and left for the river with a spring in my step that matched the confidence of my words.

It felt like that I sat forever at the edge of the river that day, but no fish were biting at all, and none were in sight. The sun shone brilliantly down on us from a deep blue sky. It was truly a glorious relaxing day filled with fun and laughter with my friends. I enjoyed fishing very much, but I was naturally sad when I found myself returning home after a day on the riverbank with nothing. I was never particularly patient, but my father taught me that God never forgets his humble servants, those who serve and honor Him well. God fills the rivers with fish for everyone. He is the provider and God will never let His servants go hungry.

As I walked back home next to the water channels which irrigated the many rice farms, I saw, to my utter amazement, four very large fish stuck in a shallow pool of water next to the one of the channels. They were unable to escape their natural cage. Without another thought, I jumped into the water and began baling the water out of the pool with my bare hands! After what seemed like ages, I had managed to empty the pool in order to retrieve the prize. I could barely contain my excitement.

While I was going home, the first stars came out. The moon did not shine at all, but the stars glittered. Crickets chirped, and frogs croaked with human voices. The darkness became heavier. Once in a while a shadow went passed me. I felt afraid. I was ready to run, then suddenly someone appeared at my side. I was shaking all over and my teeth were chattering. It was Traore. He said, "I finally found you! Your mom is worried, and sent me to find you." So Traore agreed to walk back with me.

When I was led into the house, I was so happy to be home, but I was still shaking. My mother began to wring her hands. "Woe is me! Just look at this child!" She warmed me up, and blew on me too. She recited a prayer. "Huh... no fish?" I smiled back and with pride in my voice said, "Mother, please take a look; I have brought home many gifts."

My mother hugged me tighter, her eyes glowing with so much pride and joy. She then went to the kitchen to weave her magic into cooking us a great meal. That magical find of fish fed my family and our neighbors. So many neighbors came for the meal that our small home was filled with so much joy.

Not all was so beautiful and sunny in my village. The climate was truly too hot. The land was covered by many scary beasts: serpents, scorpions, and rodents. Moreover, the people were often divided into many tribes that waged and fought bloody battles among themselves. The roads were very dangerous. Bandits hid and waited for travelers to rob, kill, or to sell them against their will. Humans were not the only lethal species in residence. There were also wild cats, dogs, boars, wolves, tigers, and lions. Some weighed in at seven hundred to eight hundred pounds, and their heads were as big as a small elephant.

There were also elephants too that weighed four or five times as much as the tigers and lions, but were of much more docile demeanor. More numerous still were the poisonous serpents, including some impressive Cobras. And then there were the rats, most of whom seemed to work for the bandits.

I recall walking to the river one day with my father at my side. The day was clear, hot and calm. Suddenly out flew his arm to stop me from taking another step. He then asked me to look down at the dirt right in front of my feet. I was confused by his words and his actions. I did not understand, but I obeyed my father, and I looked down towards the ground.

Oddly, I did not see a thing; nothing at all appeared out of the ordinary. He noticed my confused stare and replied to me, "Look at how some grains of sands are moving." My eyes focused on the sand near my feet and I realized that it was moving towards me even when there was no wind or other a reason to explain it.

My father said that there was a Njaatoldi Serpent underneath that sand, and she was waiting so patiently for us to take another step. Immediately my father and I took many steps back away from the moving sand, but our eyes stayed fixed on that spot as we regressed. With confidence and a steady hand, my father took a long stick and then touched the sand where the serpent hid. Suddenly I saw a flash of red and brown; then sand flew everywhere around me.

I could not open my eyes to see what was happening as great quantities of sand filled my face and eyes. When I was able to focus again, I was very surprised. The serpent's eyes were glaring at us, as if it was truly Satan in disguise. Rapidly, it then slithered quickly into the trees. I have seldom witnessed anything more dramatic than that moment. Such serpents often hid in the middle of the path for their prey. The serpent would wait on her back so that other animals could not see her red color. The serpent's sandy color of its belly helped its element of surprise. It laid very quietly to strike its prey. My father said God is merciful and those who love God must share his mercy with everything. Our sacred earth is our benefactor. When you walk look down so you can clearly see what you are stepping on, so not crush a bee, a flower, or even an ant.

In our village there was always talk about Satan, serpents, and spirits of the dead that do not quickly proceed to the spirit-world. My mother also spoke of demons and hobgoblins, first of all because she was interested in them, and second to frighten us children into good behavior and so we would not go astray. It is also good to remind children from time to time that there are still evil in this world. Therefore, as night came and darkness fell, fear replaced the fun and laughter of the daylight hours. That night a fierce gale blew outside. I was scared. I thought perhaps this was a sign from the Evil One, from Satan himself. The beast entered my dreams. I fell asleep, but not too well. All night, serpents haunted my dreams. Every few minutes my eyes popped open, and I would glance at the floor around me to see if Satan or his demons, or serpents were near.

I had been asleep for a few hours when I was woken by something moving next to me. My heart raced as my throat began to tighten and I gasped for breath; fear took me over. My eyes had not opened fully when I touched the ground next to the mat on which I was sleeping. Suddenly I felt my hand burning and on fire! Quickly, without realizing what had happened, I jerked my other hand towards the floor to defend myself, but instead of easing the pain, I felt the burning fire in my second arm. I jumped up and cried out in pain. My head puffed up in the darkness, and my hands burned, as if leeches were sucking up my blood and brain.

The commotion instantly woke my parents. My agony was caused by the sting of a Yahre Scorpion that had crawled next to my sleeping mat.

By the time my parents had reached my side, the scorpion had vanished between the cracks in the wall.

Yahre is a tough African Scorpion. They have developed many ways to survive. They have the ability to slow down their metabolism to allow them to survive well. This ability also allows them to shelter from the sun and heat for extended periods of time, using only little amounts of oxygen. During the rainy season the temperatures cool the earth, and the scorpions come out from under the rocks and crevices in which they hid to escape the intense summer heat. It was unfortunate for me that one crawled inside our room.

Its sting can cause excruciating pain and can be fatal, but we have been stung so many times, I guess we had built up immunity to them.

Although I was tired and my eyelids were heavy, I could not fall asleep the rest of the night. I felt as though my head was on fire. My dear mother cradled me in her arms. She recited a prayer. She lovingly gave me some water to drink and tried to cool my hands with water. My father paced back and forth. He was very upset. He chewed his beard and rubbed his head. "Dear God!" He cried out. "It is high time for our salvation." That night I did not sleep a wink. Outside, the wind howled. It blew right through the holes in the house. I was overcome by a horrible thirst. My throat was parched and burning. Every few minutes I got up for some water. My stomach throbbed and my arms ached too. By the time I fell asleep, it was morning. I did not know how long I had been asleep, a minute or an hour, but I was in pain. My body was bathed in sweat.

My head felt swollen and filled with pain, but I made an effort and sat up, but I could scarcely keep my eyes open. Time passed very slowly as the poison continued to course within my body. But after a few days the burning was gone. I was relieved that the pain had stopped and that my arms were well again. Mostly I was glad that I was well enough to go fishing again.

Excitedly, I told my mother that I was going fishing with my friends. She was delighted to see that I had recovered somewhat. She smiled at me in her loving way as I opened the door. I went outside and began to walk towards the river. A dog chased me, but I drove him off. Nothing was going to stop me from going fishing that day. But one never knows how things will turn out.

With our fishing poles, we happily ran to the river. But strange and unexpected things began to happen. All of the sudden it seemed like the sun disappeared, darkness and a foul odor enveloped the air. A storm was approaching. The howling wind knocked and banged as if with mighty hammers. Then we noticed men in a small boat. They said to run and get some villagers. "A corpse was rising from the river!" My heart plummeted fast, and my brain and eyes trembled in their sockets. A strange silence ensued. I felt a chill go through my body. A few days earlier, six people drowned during a big storm while crossing the river. Five of the bodies were recovered, but the mother's body had not. I had a dread of such things from my earliest childhood. But my curiosity was always stronger than my fears. So we ran to get help.

We knew it was the mother of the family that had come down the river to this very spot, and her body was now rising from the depths below. Our pleas brought many men to help. Events followed quickly. They respectfully took the mother out of the water. She had become very bloated from decomposition and from being in the river for so many days. They could not carry her back to the village, so they had to bury her on that spot near the river. The burial was delayed until the arrival of her son. When they placed her on the ground, her belly opened up. A seemingly endless amount of water and an odor so foul that there was nothing to compare to it in my lifetime, came out of her, but the foul odor did not affect her son at all. Still confusion, sadness, and fright were apparent in his eyes.

He held his mother in his arms with the same tenderness he had always expressed to her his entire life. Very slowly he lifted her head and kissed her forehead. Then he whispered a prayer. He did not simply whisper a prayer, but he seemed to be pleading with the Master of the Universe. I stood trembling, aghast at the son's courage. I was very torn between two conflicting feelings. My fear dictated that I turn my head the other way, but my curiosity demanded just another glance. I knew that I would pay for each glance with nightmares and torment. There were tears in my eyes. And as he wept, his tears fell on her face, then very strange events followed. Something happened so amazing that no imagination could have invented it. Her eyes opened up as if to tell him, "Do not be sad, I'm in a better place now." Upon seeing her eyes, her son's face turned pale.

A dreadful fear befell me, too. But that miracle melted the son's heart like wax. His weeping became even more intense, yet now there was in it something of joy because he was able to say goodbye. I suddenly felt dizzy. There was tightness in my chest, and an icy shudder ran down my spine. Her soul was departing. I could feel the trees around the river trembling. Her soul has gone to where all souls meet, regardless of the roles they once played in this life, in whatever tongue they spoke, and of whatever creed they followed.

My father once told me that anyone that drowns in the river goes straight up to heaven. And in the other world she will again be his mother. Though her body was there with us that day, I am certain her soul is already in heaven waiting for her son to arrive one day.

Afterward I went home. I was tired, sweating, a lost soul. That night I could not sleep at all. I napped but I awoke intermittently. Each time I fell asleep, horrors seized me. I kept thinking about the dead mother and her son. Weeks had passed, but I could not shake that overwhelming sadness. It was like the earth was torn, and I could not fix it. Then my uncle died very unexpectedly. Tears flowed endlessly from my eyes.

When a man was sick, my uncle went to comfort him. Three times a week he visited the homeless shelter, and brought them soup. He himself was poor and his poverty was etched on his kind face. From under his bushy brows gazed eyes such as only a poor man can have. Their color was black as coal. In them glowed an ancient wisdom and goodness few men have.

There was in him, great respect and reverence for every man, woman, child, and for every living creature. The saying "He would not hurt a fly" fitted him so accurately.

If a fly alighted on his nose, he would not chase it away even if it bit him. Was he, the Creator, to presume to tell a fly what to eat, or where it was permitted to land and where not? In the eyes of my uncle, my father was an angel of God, and he looked upon my mother with a mixture of awe and admiration.

Whenever he came to our house, he tried to serve my mother in some way. He would try to sweep, but mother would not permit a man of God to do such menial tasks for her.

My uncle had two passions. One was reading God's Book. Even as he sat and spoke with anyone, his sunken lips would mumble, and everyone knew that he was hurriedly reciting a verse from God's Book, or even an entire chapter or two. His second passion was soccer. His legs were bent from when he was a child so he could not play, but he loved to see the game played right. At the mere mention of soccer, tears would rise in his eyes and fall upon his beard. I cannot imagine heaven without my uncle. I cannot even conceive of a world where there is no reward for such goodness.

As we entered my uncle's house, I saw my father's face as I had never seen it before. It was flooded with so much tears. There was one gush and everything was wet, eyes, cheeks, beard.

My father took out his handkerchief to wipe his eyes and to blow his nose. In a broken voice, he said: "Sister where is our brother?" She pointed her finger towards the other room. When we entered the room, I was transfixed by what I saw. A corpse wrapped in a white sheet lay on the floor, a pair of candles at its head and my grandmother beside it on a footstool, weeping, wringing her hands, and crying out.

My ribs tingled with fright. I quickly backed outside. I began to run but became entangled in something. It was as if my dead uncle had clutched my shirt, drawing me backward. I collapsed on the ground. I threw up, and shivered. It seemed to me that I had grown too old in that one day.

After a while, a strange calm came over me, and the complete surrender that accompanies sadness so great that one knows nothing worse can occur. I do not remember how much later it was, but I know that I dozed off on the ground. I began to dream about the first time I went fishing with my uncle when I was five years old. Then I heard a noise and felt someone's touch. I opened my eyes, I saw my mother. She held me in her arms and took me home. My mother brought me some food, but I had no appetite, even though I had not eaten a thing all day.

My stomach felt bad. I fell asleep and wakened after the sun had set. For a long while my parents sat in silence. During the period of mourning, people prayed in silence and read God's Book. I prayed and I asked God to see my uncle alive once again.

I am certain that my uncle's soul was already in heaven waiting for us to arrive there one day.

The first meal of the day in our home was a far cry from the "Sugar Pops" breakfast cereal that is eaten by the rich. We ate the same non-nutritious meal every day: a piece of hard bread. When we were lucky enough to get our hands on some coffee, we would dunk the bread in it to soften it. If there was no coffee, we would often just dunk the bread in some hot water.

During the wet seasons when the Kinkeliba shrubs had leaves, the villagers would strip the branches bare, and boil the leaves in water for several hours. The result was a reddish liquid which tasted vaguely like tea. This meal, while not highly nutritious, filled our bellies.

When you are very hungry, anything remotely edible would taste good. However, there came a time when my greed got the better of me, and the bread did not taste so good. I will return to this part of the story a bit later.

One day I accepted a job working for a farmer, he gave me a few pennies in exchange for doing some chores: milking cows and mixing the milk with water. Dutifully, I handed the pennies over to my father to help pay for food. I was under the impression that my contribution would entitle me to a larger piece of bread the next morning.

Perhaps I would even be able to set aside a little extra for a snack later in the day when my stomach was growling with hunger.

Naturally, I was wrong; my father gave me the same amount of bread as he gave everyone else.

"I do not want to eat this awful bread again!" I blustered.

"Where was my extra portion?"

"Why was there nothing better to eat than this bread? "

I had not considered the fact that there was simply nothing else to eat. It was a tough lesson I had to learn. The only way to survive in the place that we lived was by sharing. Everyone had to contribute in whatever manner they were able.

In return, everyone got the same amount of whatever we had. In this way, my family was able to give each member something to eat every day.

My father sat motionless. He was visibly upset. In his eyes there was so much sadness. For a long time there was a heavy silence in the house. Father stood, his face pale, and shook his head. My brothers and sisters stared at each other. They were confused and perplexed. There was, obviously, no more to be said, nothing further to be argued. My father said, "Drink your tea and give the bread to your brother." Before I had time to react at all, my youngest brother Abraham snapped the bread away from me and ate it.

Mother ran into the kitchen to weep unseen. Father stood for a while in a corner and wiped some tears from his eyes. Often after breakfast, father would ask each of us children a question and how we are doing, but this time all remained silent.

I paid so dearly for speaking before considering the costs. I realized that I had done something very wrong. I felt contemptuous of myself. I made a resolution that day to which I still follow: never put money above God and family, and never do anything for money that goes against the grain. I wanted to relieve myself as soon as possible from that miserable job. Adulterating milk is punished by a fine and imprisonment too.

My father taught me that one should avoid sin at all costs, but there is a way of rectifying an error. Man must do what lies in his power, and he must rely upon God, because no evil comes from Him.

For days a sad silence hung over our house. Father lingered over his prayers in his corner of the house. He no longer chatted much.

Once, however, I heard him say that he had only one request to make of God: that he might no longer have to earn his living as a farm hand. Rain had not fallen for some sixty days, and he could not find work. I frequently heard him sigh his familiar sigh and whisper the plea: "Ah, woe is us, dear God ..." And he would then add: "How much longer? I knew what my father meant: how much longer will this bitter life last? And how much longer until the rains come?

Then, as if in response to my daily prayers, everyone began to speak to me once again. Everyone was very gracious. Slowly we began to forget the incident. And the shame that I felt diminished.

Dad once again smiled and became approachable, and he began to tell us stories and to repeat his lore. The bread actually tasted very good, but the quality of our bread was such that even though it looked normal, clean it was not. Anyone who saw the bread maker making the bread would not eat it at all. The fact of the matter is that making bread is a very strenuous task. As the bread maker kneaded the dough, his body would excrete lots of sweat and his nose would run. These fluids would then fall into the dough. He often sneezed too from all the flour dust and the spittle from his mouth would fall in as well! The truth is that each bread maker gave their own sweat and flavor to their bread from their bodily excretions. Everyone in my village were used to it, and no one was upset. Somehow we lived through that exposure.

I was hungry for most of that day, but because fasting was part of my life, I was able to make it through the day without major hardships. That day was no worse than many other days that I had faced. Long ago, I had discovered that a human being requires very little to survive. A half cup of milk and a piece of dry bread can suffice for an entire day.

There were times when we ate some leaves to ease the hunger pains, and to stop the annoying growling noises that came from our bellies. At other times we were even more creative. We would take a stone that had been baking in the hot sun for hours, wrap it in a cloth and then place the cloth and the warm stone around our belly so that we would not feel the hunger pains. The warmth was soothing and distracted us from thinking about food for a while.

The weekends always had a holiday-like quality in our house, especially in the winter-time. As I slept, I could smell all sorts of seasonings and aromas traveling quickly to my nose. My mother's cooking was the best. As I dreamt about food, I heard a tempestuous knocking on the outside door.

Father was alarmed. Mother looked upset. I jumped out of my bed. No one had ever knocked on our door this early. Knocking with such force and anger for us could mean only one thing—trouble, the Berber Nazi Police! Then we heard screams of joy coming from outside. I opened my eyes very wide, then I ran outside to see to my amazement, our neighbor was truly almost naked and dancing around the cooking fire. He had even thrown his shirt and pants into the fire.

He looked at me and smiled and said to do the same. He said I will buy you a new shirt. I wrongly assumed that he was simply overjoyed that the rains had come during the night, but I was very wrong. The story behind his joy was quite different. He had just arrived home from working about 400 miles away in Senegal. In Senegal, people often bet on horse races that actually took place in France. He had placed a bet on one of the races. On the way home from Senegal he heard that he had won. When he saw his wife, he showed her the winning ticket and his promise of money to come-and then he placed the ticket in his pocket. Soon his family all began to dance happily around the fire. The entire family had been infected by the same fever. Here, life was presenting a happy drama more exciting than those one finds in the newspapers.

Our neighbor did not win millions, but the few thousands of francs or dollars he did win, would buy him and his family fish and bread for a few years. It was very hard not to feel his excitement. I was about to take off my shirt and throw it in the fire, when I glanced towards my father for his permission. My father shook his head and I understood.

My neighbor looked at my father and me and smiled. No more torn shirts. No more scorpions biting those bare feet. Our neighbor then went in circles curiously touching his chest and sides. We thought that was part of the happy dance, but he was looking for the ticket. Suddenly he screamed and leapt towards the fire, burning his hands trying to extract his shirt from the flames. It was too late.

With all the excitement and joy he had thrown his shirt with the ticket in its pocket into the fiery blaze. Our neighbor fell on his knees to the ground weeping. My father told me to run home and get his new shirt and pants that mother had sewn for my dad. It did not take too long for my father to make our neighbor smile again. He invited him and his family to come eat with us. It was a crazy, unusual day, but by the end of it, everyone had eaten well and was happy. Even our hapless neighbor was smiling and had forgotten about his misfortune with the lost winning horse race ticket.

It was a summer evening. My father had just come home from working a long day. We were sitting eating our dinner: rice boiled in some milk. The door was open. A light breeze blew in from the outside, bringing with it a hint of bread and smoke.

The bakers had just lit the ovens for baking tomorrow's bread. Suddenly, Berber soldiers burst into our house and dragged us outside. Then they lit our house on fire. The Nazis burned everything: chairs, benches, prayer books, papers, blankets were aflame. My youngest brother quickly fetched water from the well and tried to extinguish the flames, but with unbelievable brutality they dragged him and beat him over his head. My father ran to help, but they whipped him well. Man was descended from an ape, I once heard. I never thought it was true till I saw the Nazis today. A border dispute over farming rights sent Mauritania and Senegal on a collision course to war. The Berbers feared that the Africans might unite to defeat them, so they executed thousands of black Mauritanians in their army, and threw thousands of people into the river to drown.

The soldiers confiscated everything with value that they could get their hands on, like documents, money, jewelry, so no survivors could claim that they were Mauritanians.

I still remember that day as though it had been yesterday. I opened my eyes and saw many flames large and small ones, rolling from one house to next, and dancing like Satan's imps. Then we were thrown to die in the river.

The Senegalese people living near the river ran to help. They pulled us from the water and gave us what little clothing and blankets they had to try and warm us up. The villagers even stripped off items of their own clothing and handed them to us, expecting nothing in return. They gave us their food to eat and a place to sleep.

In return, we only stayed in their village for about seven days. The village was small, and very short on supplies, and since there were thousands of us refugees, we did not want to tax their lives any more than necessary.

We traveled to some empty fields, and set up a camp. The government was kind at the beginning, and sent us some tents. Life was truly tough, but for some reason we survived; perhaps so that I might tell my story.

It is difficult to tell you everything. Life in the camp was incredibly hard. I thought to myself: Can a young boy survive in such an abyss? Can a boy confined to such a sordid place keep his sanity? I suddenly felt a tightness in my chest and an icy shudder ran down my back.

Everyone's life became increasingly difficult, but somehow we survived. To this day, I still do not understand how. When we arrived at the camp, all we had were the donated clothes on our backs. There were no mats, and so every night we slept on the bare dirt. We had no food at all. So at night I dreamt about food, and even the dogs barked of hunger too.

As the refugee camp began to fill up with more refugees, it got harder and harder to find even basic necessities like firewood for cooking. I had to walk for several hours to find a small pile of twigs. Everyone became very acquainted with hunger. I saw that the skin hung very loosely on my neighbor's pale face. But his young sons, were even paler and more emaciated.

Even though I was only a little boy then, and I could not read or write, I understood the difficult nightmare that we were in. Many times in the past I had wished the impossible to happen, and God Almighty made it happen. But where was God now? I wondered.

The days were interminable. And I was filled with many questions but no one wanted to answer them. So I took my questions to the river to ponder alone. "How long am I going to be here?" I asked. "Probably, for an eternity plus a day," I answered myself.

I grew accustomed to being so alone and answering my own questions. I began to question if God did exist. If He did, why does He let so many bad things happen? I waited for a sign from Him, but there was no answer.

My thoughts kept going to the past. I found myself thinking about Traore and Lemine. Where were they now? Were they in good spirit? Or are they resting, martyred by the Nazis. Do they ever think of me? Or had they risen into spheres where they were no longer concerned with this life? I started to pray for them, and I invited them to visit me on this river bank to fish one last time.

Suddenly I heard a noise. I thought God Almighty must have heard my prayers, but it was a mouse. I had not seen any animals at all since we arrived. But I did see birds that flew high overhead in swarms. Butterflies of all colors fluttered above the river: red, yellow, brown, with all kinds of dots and patterns. The air smelled of earth here, of dirt and grass. Still there was strange stillness, and yet everything murmured and chirped. Blossoms fell from somewhere and settled on my head and shoulders. I looked up at the sky, saw the sun, the clouds high above, and suddenly the little mouse came closer and closer to me. I held my breath very tightly. I said to her, "Do not worry. No harm will come to you." She watched me intently. I threw a piece of dry bread. Slowly she began gnawing the bread. Then she cocked her head and gave me a sidelong glance, as if she was asking, "Where have you been all my life? I was very hungry for a long time. What does she think about all day? I asked myself. She must think about something. The mouse does have a brain, a mind, and a nervous system as us humans. She is just as much a part of God's creation as the stars, the moon, and the sun. She suddenly raised her tiny head and starred at me with a look of love and gratitude. I imagined that she was saying thank you for the bread.

For my father the answer to every question was always God. But how did he know there was a God, since no one saw Him? But if He did not exist, who had created the sun, the moon, the stars, the trees, the birds, and this world? And what happened when my uncle died? Is heaven real? Or was a dead person no better off than a dead fish. I do not recall a time when these questions did not torment me well.

The nights were pitch black, and icy. The cold was truly awful. No amount of covering sufficed. The howling wind knocked and banged terribly. The tents felt like a ship floating on an ocean of sand. The wind, rustling through the tall sand dune grasses, made me think of serpents and imps.

Huddled next to my father, cold and afraid, I dreamt that I flew over my old village. These were not dreams but visions. I hovered over churches, temples, and mosques. I saw funeral processions, Nazis, and monsters. But I was not afraid, God Almighty was holding me in His Mighty Hand.

I dreamt that I was Prophet Joseph. God gave me so much food, I threw them open in the seven years of famine, and everyone ate. Then a word from me made the Nazis tremble in their boots, as well as their generals and all the soldiers and kings that came after them. I drew my sword and I finished them all off. I took hold of their souls in my hand and, accompanied by a band of angles, flew them all to hell and the nether world.

Before the war, I used to buy some sugar candy several times a month. Here, sugar is a luxury no one can afford, not to mention cooking oil. Sardines were a real treat when we got them. From time to time we would receive tins of sardines and dried awful fish in aide parcels from the outside world. However, the dried fish were extra rubbery, and as salty as the sea. No matter how hard I chewed on them, I could not seem to swallow it down. Still everyone ate extra sparingly so that the fish lasted several days.

One day, an old woman came to our tent and asked my father if we had some sardines that we could spare. She said her children had been crying for days because they were hungry. She had borrowed some rice and wanted to mix some sardines with it.

Father called out to mother: "Please give me the sardines that you have, quickly!"

"How much do you need?"

"As much as you have."

Mother was very upset.

"But what about our little children? I cannot give away everything!"

"I beg of you, do not keep this poor woman waiting."

Tears rose to my eyes. And with trembling fingers, mother took out all the sardines. She had grown pale.

Without another word, my father gave the old woman all the sardines that we had. The woman asked, "Are you sure?"

My father replied, "God will not forget us." My father then asked me to collect some firewood. I wandered along the path with the children, daydreaming of the time I used to spend fishing back home.

Every morning as the sun began its slow crawl up the sky, we would wake up to work in the millet fields. When the weeding and watering were finished, we would head off to collect firewood to sell, and for that day's cooking as well. These were good times, filled with laughter and horseplay in the fields and forests.

I remember one day my mother said to keep an eye on my baby sister while she went to borrow some hot coals for our cooking fire. My sister was about two years old, and was playing quietly in the shade of a large tree. Suddenly, I heard loud rustling in the branches above, and my heart was in my mouth. My mind skipped through a list of the various animals it could be – a lion, a tiger, a monkey – which were all far bigger and stronger than I was. But, it was a Gundo which jumped out of the tree, landing next to my sister. A Gundo is a very rare lizard. It is immense, but of little physical threat because of its vegetarian diet of fruits and flowers. Many people in my village believed that they would become rich if they eat part of a Gundo, so this poor lizard was hunted to the brink of extinction. Our neighbor had heard my sister's surprised cry, and came running to help. When he saw the Gundo, the neighbor thought he had won the lottery again. He took a flying leap, desperately trying to grasp hold of the treasure. The Gundo whipped his long tail around, slapping my neighbor hard on the backside.

My neighbor fell flat on his face, jumping up just in time to see the Gundo escaping to the tops of the trees. Furious, he bellowed to the heavens, "I'll catch you next time, Gundo! I promise I will catch you and eat you!"

The Gundo had frightened me a little but it was a beautiful animal, and I knew I was lucky to see one alive; I was happy my neighbor hadn't been able to eat it. I turned away so my neighbor couldn't see me laughing at his farcical defeat and the Gundo's underhanded victory.

I was jolted from my daydream as we came upon a large tree, under which lay some dead wood. I was reaching out a hand to pick up some wood, to my astonishment, I saw a beautiful Gundo sitting on its eggs.

That made me smile, as memories of our old home and our neighbor flooded my head again.

Just as the Gundo was protecting her brood below her body, so my mother used to protect us all, enveloping us with her love and encouragement.

Of course, if the other children had seen the Gundo, they would have killed it and eaten it, and cooked its eggs. I needed a distraction fast. Without thinking about it, I yelled, "Snake!" The children shrieked loudly and scampered back towards the camp. They ran smack into an old woman, and she heard them yell "Snake! Snake!" To my amazement, the old woman grinned, and began trotting towards me. Darn! I had forgotten that some old women think snake is a delicacy, desiring it even more than chicken.

The Gundo was in trouble, and I had no clue what to do next. I scrunched my eyes shut and began to pray. "Please God help!" I could not help but feel a deepening sadness for this Gundo. Though my people may believe that eating a Gundo will bring wealth and prosperity, just seeing the Gundo alive is the true treasure. At that moment I heard a cry, "Food!" I thought the old woman had found the Gundo. I opened my eyes slowly, preparing for a grisly scene. Instead, I was shocked to see that everyone were running away from me, and the old woman had stumbled and fell to the ground. I saw a rich Mauritanian man and his sons standing next to a big horse-drawn wagon, handing out bread. There was food for everyone! Even the old woman was now trundling her way towards the man, the sure source of food.

In my country we have a saying that says, "God is always very near, and responds to prayers, especially in difficulty or an emergency." God had answered my prayers; the Gundo and her eggs were safe.

Even as I write this, many years later, I have to smile. I ran towards the wagon too. To my amazement, the wagon was full of bread, fish and fruits.

On the days that our bellies were content, this kind Mauritanian man and his family and sons were always responsible. We were very close to starvation. He alone saved our lives. It took tremendous courage to stand up, speak out, and act against the powers that be. This man was risking his own safety by associating with us and giving us food.

Thousands of refugees continued to move from one country to the next. But we continued to hear news of him from time to time. One son died, a daughter fell in love with a young Nazi Berber Soldier. Her father was deeply grieved. A few weeks later, I read among the obituaries that the father died. He was buried, but no city was given.

May these memoirs of him serve as a monument to him and his like, who lived in sanctity and died as martyrs.

Good Reads

Quran in Color	ISBN 9781643543987
Quran in Color	ISBN 9781643543994
Stories of the Prophets	ISBN 9781643544977
Stories of the Prophets	ISBN 9781643543703
Stories of the Qur'an	ISBN 9781643544991
Khalid Bin Al-Waleed	ISBN 9781643543437
Quran in English	ISBN 9781643543543
Don't Be Sad! Be Happy	ISBN 9781643544878

Noah's Stories of the Prophets - Bible and Torah
ISBN 9781643544847

Timeless Seeds of Advice for the Muslima
ISBN 9781643544472

The Ídeal Muslímah   ISBN 9781643544458

Timeless Seeds of Advice to a Friend
ISBN 9781643544359

Muhammad: The Best Human Being of all Time
ISBN 9781643544342

Al-Husain Ibn Ali	ISBN 9781643544328
The Friends of Allah	ISBN 9781643544236
Gardens of Purification	ISBN 9781643544229
The Spiritual Cure	ISBN 9781643544212
Fleeing From the Fire	ISBN 9781643544205

www.ingramcontent.com/pod-product-compliance
Lightning Source LLC
Chambersburg PA
CBHW072133070526
44585CB00016B/1660